HAUNTED PLACES

HAUNTED BATTLEFIELDS

KENNY ABDO

Fly!
An Imprint of Abdo Zoom
abdobooks.com

abdobooks.com

Published by Abdo Zoom, a division of ABDO, P.O. Box 398166, Minneapolis, Minnesota 55439. Copyright © 2021 by Abdo Consulting Group, Inc. International copyrights reserved in all countries. No part of this book may be reproduced in any form without written permission from the publisher. Fly!™ is a trademark and logo of Abdo Zoom.

Printed in the United States of America, North Mankato, Minnesota.
052020
092020

Photo Credits: Alamy, AP Images, iStock, Newscom, Shutterstock,
Production Contributors: Kenny Abdo, Jennie Forsberg, Grace Hansen
Design Contributors: Dorothy Toth, Neil Klinepier

Library of Congress Control Number: 2019956158

Publisher's Cataloging-in-Publication Data

Names: Abdo, Kenny, author.
Title: Haunted battlefields / by Kenny Abdo
Description: Minneapolis, Minnesota : Abdo Zoom, 2021 | Series: Haunted places | Includes online resources and index.
Identifiers: ISBN 9781098221300 (lib. bdg.) | ISBN 9781644944110 (pbk.) | ISBN 9781098222284 (ebook) | ISBN 9781098222772 (Read-to-Me ebook)
Subjects: LCSH: Haunted places--Juvenile literature. | Battlefields--Juvenile literature. | Ghosts--Juvenile literature. | Soldiers--Juvenile literature.
Classification: DDC 133.122--dc23

TABLE OF CONTENTS

Battlefields 4

The History 8

The Haunted 12

The Media 20

Glossary 22

Online Resources 23

Index 24

BATTLEFIELDS

History's biggest battles claimed lives all over the world. Today, those ghosts of war are said to still march across the hallowed battlefields where they fought.

Every major war has been studied for decades. But many people don't know the **supernatural** happenings that have plagued the grounds since.

Battlefields are the location for most confrontations and general warfare.

Battles can break out in any location where two rival forces face each other. However, some battlefield locations were agreed upon beforehand.

Today, battlefields are considered shrines to those lost in war. But, there is something paranormal lurking throughout these grounds.

11

THE HAUNTED

The **Wars of the Roses** lasted more than 30 years. In the Battle of Towton, nearly 30,000 people died while fighting in a snowstorm. A similar snowstorm goes through Towton every few years. Some have seen the battle rage on through the snow.

Gettysburg is the most famous battle of the American Civil War. There were more than 50,000 casualties. After 150 years, visitors have reported seeing spirits roaming the fields.

The **Battle of Cold Harbor** lasted two weeks. Confederate and Union armies fought nonstop. Today, the battlefield is known as one of the most haunted sites in America. Some can still smell the gunpowder.

The **Battle of Little Bighorn** was fought during the **Great Sioux War**. The Lakota tribe defeated the United States Calvary. Today, some claim to experience visions of the battle while visiting the site.

Nearly 500,000 soldiers died in the **Battle of Passchendaele**. The village in Belgium is said to be very haunted. Some say they hear sounds of gunfire and screams that belong to no one.

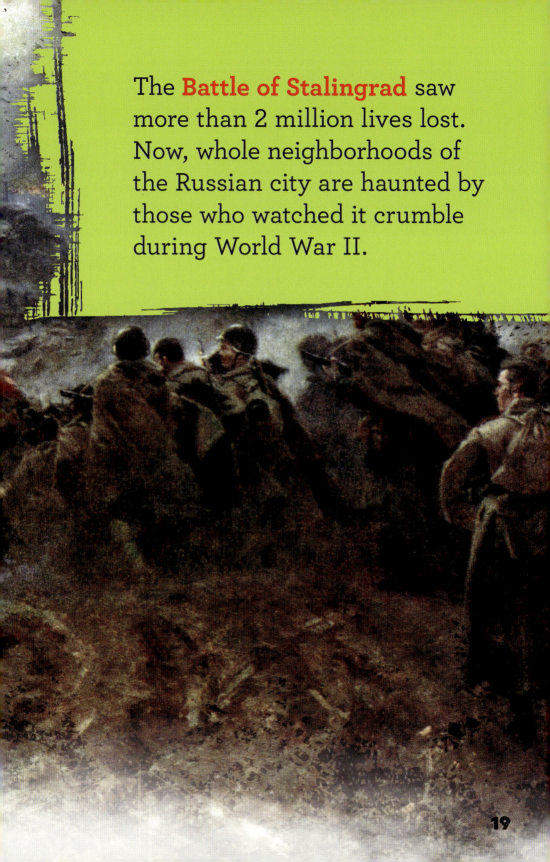

The **Battle of Stalingrad** saw more than 2 million lives lost. Now, whole neighborhoods of the Russian city are haunted by those who watched it crumble during World War II.

THE MEDIA

There are many books and documentaries about haunted battlefields. Horror movies and TV shows highlight the eeriness of these locations.

Guided tours offer nighttime scares to those brave enough. Anyone who goes and survives has a spooky story to share for life…or death.

GLOSSARY

Battle of Cold Harbor – (May – June of 1864) Considered one of the bloodiest battles of the Civil War.

Battle of Gettysburg – (July 1-3 of 1863) It had the largest number of deaths in the entire Civil War.

Battle of Little Bighorn – (June 25-26 of 1876) Around 259 US soldiers and about 30 native Americans died.

Battle of Passchendaele – a World War I fight that lasted more than three months. More than 500,000 soldiers died.

Battle of Stalingrad – the largest battle of World War II. It lasted more than five months.

Great Sioux War – battles between the Lakota Sioux, North Cheyenne, and United States. It lasted for one year.

supernatural – a force beyond scientific logic and the laws of nature.

Wars of the Roses – a series of English civil wars for the throne of England.

ONLINE RESOURCES

To learn more about haunted battlefields, please visit abdobooklinks.com or scan this QR code. These links are routinely monitored and updated to provide the most current information available.

INDEX

American Civil War 14, 15

Battle of Cold Harbor 15

Battle of Gettysburg 14

Battle of Little Bighorn 16

Battle of Passchendaele 17

Battle of Stalingrad 19

Battle of Towton 13

Great Sioux War 16

haunted tours 21

media 20

Native American tribes 16

Wars of the Roses 13